The Gifted Quiet
Poems & Performance Words

RiShana Blake

A Literary Lorene Book

The Gifted Quiet: Poems and Performance Words

Blake, RiShana
The Gifted Quiet / RiShana Blake
ISBN: 978-0-9835699-7-8
First printing

Cover design by James Carter

Library of Congress Control Number: 2011910606

Published by
Literary Lorene
P. O. Box 1282
Long Island City, NY 11101
http: www.LiteraryLorene.com

Dedication

This book is for my students who develop and express their opinions on religion, politics, sexuality and a host of other topics, and who find voices to candidly speak in the presence of their peers.

Table of Contents

Remembering Rosa

The Meeting - 1
A plus - 2
Millennium Chatter Box - 3
At the Premier - 4
Summer 1955 - 7
Funeral - 8
In Flight - 9
A Soldier in the Army of the Lord – 10

Portraits of Mama

Snow Cream - 13
Down Shirley Durham's Lane - 15
The Remedy - 17
Mommy and Ma - 19
Wild Fro - 20
Lockologist - 22
Two Writers Writing - 23
Are you happy? - 24
Back In Texas – 25

Silent Strength

Aileytude - 27
Morning Prayer - 28
For the rabbit that screams - 29
As ferocious as a lion - 30
Rain - 31
Flower girl - 32
unorthodox man - 33
Redemption - 34
I am - 36

Portraits of a Woman Relating

Moon-woman - 37
Feline Friend - 38
Feeling like - 40
Katrina Unfinished - 41
Slipped - 42
Colette - 43
Confidence - 45
Church-hopping - 47
Restless - 48
Shhh! Don't Talk About That! - 49
Wrapped Attention - 51
Beer - 52
Star Stuck - 53

Confused Blue - 55
Healing Time - 56
Metamorphose – 57
Pleasure - 58
Ode to Ice Cream - 59

Morning Psalms

Tremble - 61
Tender - 62
Commune - 63
Open - 64
Nation - 65
Inequity - 66
Trust - 67
Sing - 68
Marvel - 69
Path- 70
Within Me - 71
Restore – 72
Salvation - 73
Praise – 74
A New Song – 75

Remembering Rosa

The Meeting

I was seven, Rosa Parks,
and my spirit saluted you
the moment you walked
into our living room.

Excited, I refused sleep,
begging to miss curfew
and lie at your feet. Grace
removed the pedestal

and I fell in love with
the person behind scenes
of the Montgomery boycott;
fame faded into humanity.

You were like grandma
and, I one of your girls,
with a hushed laughter
tickling my little world.

I held on to the memory
of you cooking with us
and for the rest of your life
saw you and made no fuss.

A Plus

I did a report on you,
and I got an "A."
I puffed out one sentence
and you smiled.
My heart boomed--
me and my "A"
in the dining room
with you, Mother Rosa.

Millennium Chatter Box

My lips vibrate endlessly
Without reason--out of season,
Catching cold it makes me sick;
I stutter on my own rhetoric,

The vulnerable, talkative!

How soothing it would be
To learn the art of Rosa Parks,
The gifted quiet that incites riots
And makes soldiers leap.

Her wisdom is what I seek.

Yet, I slip, slide and soak
In speech, fast and flippant;
My mouth got me on this rope.
I'm loud and yet I'm choked.

At the Premier,
I walk the carpet with the executives.
A rope of red divides the crowd from us.
They rush, and clamor; cheers they give.
Premiering *Rosa Parks* creates indeed a fuss.
A made-for-television special—true,
but Angela Basset is playing her.
My favorite actress always makes me groove.
Will she come up to Harlem—pierce my world?
She is a superstar; will she appear?
An invited friend from home joins me; we chill.
She blends with producers gets their ear.
"Oh girl," she says to me, "she'll show, she will.
Let's rub elbows, hobnob, enjoy hors d'oeuvres."
I grab crabmeat on toast in little curves.

I grab crabmeat on toast in little curves,
and crave popcorn and soda too,
but popcorn shrimp is jauntily served
by waiters dressed in tux—impressive crew.
Is this the movies—so bourgeoisie bad,
a haughty horde of beautiful people?
With scenes like this I take a polite pass.
If not for Rosa I'd leave on the double,
but here I sit listening to idle chatter.
"So what do you do for a living, girl?"
I think, *To you, does it really matter*?
He plays who's who. I give the game a swirl.
"Oh, I just work with youth around this town."
I tell the man in slacks and button downs.

I tell the man in slacks and button downs
about the little job I do for youth
and head for the crab cakes passing 'round.
"You work for youth? My-my, is that the truth?
You have the most important job in here.
That is what Rosa Parks did too!"
He bellows as he walks away. I stare,
my heart swelling with pride. I am the kid
compared to the queen bee, Rosa Parks.
This whole event is in honor of her life.
The lady creates a swarm, summons the stars.
I scan the scene again and pinch myself twice,
Then mingle warmly. In walks Angela Basset
Would I have the courage to be *sasseey*?

Would I have the courage to be *sasseey*?
"Hi, I want to say hello to you because
it's rare to meet an artist who has had
profound effect on my life by standing tall."
Amazing, my words spill over the backs
of five women between her and me. I fail
at keeping cool, but as a worshipper—no slack.
"Oh, hello," she is friendly. I want to sail
into the theater but stop, plant my feet firmly
on the ground. *This is ridiculous*, I scold myself.
She loves Rosa; after all she did this movie.
I'm an actor. Okay, not famous like her but I help
the youth—the most important job in here.
I calm myself with this reason to cheer.

I calm myself with this reason to cheer:
I help the youth. Like the Rosa and Raymond
Institute, I dedicate my service.

Summer 1955

Coldest summer the south sees:
Emmett's mother mourns with a protest.
An open casket funeral graces
the cover of Jet Magazine.
"Show my boy with his head
swollen," five times the size
of normalcy. America, this is
her protest 'cause *She who believes*
in freedom shall not rest.

Climate of the south is guided
not by weather, but by racial intensity.
In December, a rising heat explodes in
Rosa, who expresses her fatigue. Led
by her God, she loses her inner peace.
Defiant, she faces the justice system in
Montgomery and moves toward racial
equality with a quiet strength, a new way
to fight: the refusal to give up her seat
leads her to jail, 'cause *She who believes*
in freedom shall not rest.

Martin Luther King followed by Malcolm X,
Like Emmett, face premature deaths. Coretta
and Betty, widows who live for the dream,
raise their children but Betty burns. Both
women do their best 'cause *She who believes*
in freedom shall not rest.

Funeral

My mother eyes are crimson cracked.
She writes the obituary, while I sleep,
then irons Rosa's dress, pressed.

Her daughter[1] works in darkness
to give enlightenment, then rises
without ceremony to list guests

and arrange flowers. No detail is
too small, no task too great to make
sure Rosa goes home okay that day.

It's a mystery to me how these women
labor silently. Can only I see how much
Rosa Parks meant to them, how they grieve?

---

[1]Mrs, Parks often referred to her longtime friend and executive
assistant, Elaine Steele, as her daughter.

In flight

Eternal friends:
Martin, Malcolm and Mamie speak.
Martin is frustrated; calls racism a disease;
Malcolm ponders the rippling effects of HIV
as they huddle around me in reverie.
"Rosa, Rosa, have another cup of tea,"
Mamie, Emmitt Tills' mother, sweetly says.
While we reminisce about our earthly days,
"Emmitt walks in quick-paced;
throws his arms 'round my waist.
"Emmitt!" I exclaim. Mamie smiles;
beautiful is the face of her child.
"Aunt Rosa," he asks, "is it true that today,
people use the N-word in a friendly way?"
He wants to settle a longstanding debate
with my beloved Institute[2] son, Faluke,
who drowned on a Pathways to Freedom ride.
Faluke greets me with hugs. I flutter with pride.
Then, drumbeats open heaven for me:
"Raymond!" I blush. He gently strokes my face,
holds my hand, pulls me into his space.

---

[2]The Rosa and Raymond Parks Institute for Self-Development was founded by Mrs. Parks and Ms. Steele to help youth reach their full potential. One of its premier programs is the Pathways to Freedom Tours.

A Soldier in the Army of the Lord

(For Dr. McIntosh on the first anniversary of Rosa Parks' home-going)

Then there is this moment
when it seems we can't go on.
Choked with fear and insecure,
looks like we've lost our pride,
but one million chant at my side.
I climb the stage, sing my song—
A Soldier in the Army of the Lord.

Repeated failed tries,
segregation
didn't cut my cord.
Battles! I've cried,
but my spirit is strong—
A soldier in the Army of the Lord.

Some people don't realize,
Some people don't see
that massive God
that lives in me
and they are amazed
the way I heal pain
through quiet strength.
Tonight I laugh;
my soul is free.
I celebrate another year;

death did not conquer me—
A soldier in the Army of the Lord.

Watch your step;
the sword is swinging.
Racism will get checked.
This ain't about pride
It's *My Story*.
Tellin' you 'bout my ride
and how I've come to be—
A soldier in the Army of the Lord
who saved me.

Portraits of Mama

Snow Cream

Blue birds perch in trees,
flutter and flicker in the freeze,
a powdered sugar scene.

I watch from the window.

In Mama's hand,
the silver serving spoon
sways to swipe snow.
Cradling the crock,
she packs it tight.

Black galoshes left at the door,
in brown cotton stockings
she shuffles in slides
to the kitchen.

Gardenia-sweet
condensed milk, vanilla
extract, pinches of sugar
whipped into a frost.

I lick the spoon and tingle.

Before acid rain concerns,
aerosol can contamination,
or smog, anything hazy was fog.
Snow lay in its pristine beauty,
unpolluted.

"Mama more cream," I beg.
"You'll get a sore throat," she says.

I lick the crock too.

Down Shirley Durham's Lane

No address,
no street sign--
down the dirt road
into the woods
unmarked--
we know it
by sight:
Shirley Durham's Lane.

On the right,
shack one:
the Tarpley's place
sits on an open plot
exposed like the
rough spots of
an elephant's butt.
Mary Tarpley
leans against an
ax handle at
the wood-chopping stump,
Her short hair is crimped and
nails bit to the quick are
painted a Christmas red.
I want to visit, but

Shirley Durham's Lane
hops the creek,
climbs the hill.

Shack two:
Miss Almeda's
morning glories
shade her porch.
I swing and
munch a teacake.
Miss Almeda
and Mama talk.
Our stop at the
half-way point
refreshes but...

The lane beckons
down the sandy
road to a dead-end
of spindly pines
and shack three:
our house,
shaped like an "L,"
and weather-beaten.
Furniture
is sparse, but
warmth glows from
the ABCs that
Mama and I have
cut from cardboard,
colored with crayons,
and tacked on the walls
of the front room,
down Shirley Durham's Lane.

The Remedy

Grandma,
queen of the kitchen,
whipped up a batch
of cornbread, while
field peas simmered
in the pot
but I was hungry,
and hurried to the porch.
"Grandpa, I got a headache,"
I whined. "Hun, gimme sum
a dat *anti-pain* oil," he called
out to Grandma.

I loved the sweetness
in the red bottle,
anti-pain oil. I took
a teaspoon—sweet
to the tongue.
She got it from
the Hadacol Man,
that had all his goods
in a T-model Ford.

Grandma was a root woman,
like Eve.
On the days I was sick
she boiled pine needles
with sugar to make

pine-top tea. I drank happy.
The sweetness drove
pain away.

Dried droppings the size of
a saucer or dinner plate--
cow chips. Grandma swore
they had an instant cure.
And they did, 'cause
I was cured the minute
she said, "Try a lil' bit of
dis' cow-chip tea."

Mommy and Ma

We are the tulips of Bessie's backyard.
You're vivacious violet; I'm rousing red.
Blooming brilliant in our seasons,
We bud out of one plant.

Violet: October, 1964 a star is born.
Mommy is basement parties, puffing cigarettes,
Vodka in the freezer, drunken husband scorned,
Aristotle all-knowing girl, mod squad dressed.

Red: June, 1975 a pure light arrives.
Ma is bible studies, smoking quit,
an adult-education innovator,
the sober married woman, paying the rent.

In our names sketches of her life:
Kanari means star; RiShana, a pure light;
Bessie, a place where God dwells.

Wild 'Fro (A song for Mama)

I'm a yellow rose on the north side
trying to find my way among city girls.
Baby I'm not scared of the big cars
and polluted air won't flop my curls
because

My locks swing free—I don't sweat
summer, muggy murmuring. I will
take you back to your roots. The blown
out hair is haunted, so naturally,
I twist.

And, every day when walking
I say hello to every John Doe
I meet in the streets. And, at night
'fore I close my eyes, I pray
just in case; that's what Mama
taught me. But, by sunrise I'm
singing in the shower, got power
because,

My locks swing free—I don't sweat
summer, muggy murmuring. I will
take you back to your roots. The blown
out hair is haunted, so naturally,
I twist.

Now I'm home frying chicken,
whipping up cornbread to relax
my head from my 9-5. And
kids are playin' kick the can
outside my window. It ain't simple.
The cars are honking. But, by sunset, I'm
singing in the shower, my power,
because,

My locks swing free—I don't sweat
summer, muggy murmuring, I will
take you back to your roots. The blown
out hair is haunted, so naturally,
I twist.

My locks swing free—I don't sweat
summer, muggy murmuring, I will
take you back to your roots.

Lockologist

Perfect parted symmetry, coconut oil
glossing my scalp. Elegance lifted from the
experience. Having been coiled into
beautiful, I forget

the cost. I'm not chemically treated—a lye!
I carry out appointments, "touching up" locks
ten times a year. Arrogance is washed in my
head; conditioned, I dry.

Lockologist, capturing unruly strands,
I need you 'cause vanity is chief in me.
So I end up spending more money to maintain
What could come naturally.

Two Writers Writing

A writer
telling her story
is a torturous treat.
She, the subject,
edits and re-writes
each scene.
I want
the narrative,
so won't quit.
I try
to hear it
from the
beginning,
but she
writes on.
I might
share her
story
in songs--
mixing melodies
with words,
use this venue
to describe
the life of a
heavy-headed
hushed woman
who writes
in her talk.

Are you happy?

I can grip it:
reality,
no fairytale.
We'll not tussle
in the kitchen.
My belly's big.
It's time to change
diapers and you don't
dote over me.
Years earlier,
you left. Now
in a trance, I
dream of lusty
love.

Calm, a lack
of disturbance,
Joy comes with-
in. Chasing it is
useless. Just write;
zip down the roads
of East Texas.
It's easy to
get from here to
happy.

Back in Texas

I wasn't looking for a place,
but longing for a place in time.

Smithland had changed:
no outhouses,
no kerosene lamps
no horse-drawn carriages
no sandbed roads--
everything went electric.

Aunt Minnie was dead.
Aunt TooToo was dead.
Grandpa was dead.
Grandma was old;
she was boiling
the dish rag in the peas.
She was putting bacon in
her peach cobbler.

I can't go backwards,
but I can go inside;
maybe there I will
find home.

Silent Strength

Aileytude

Broadway star, classically trained: "five, six
seven, eight." Let's arabesque to hip-hop beats;
mix up the scene. West Africans, plié! Russians,
pop and lock! *Attitude* Alvin—no shoes, just feet.

A revelation kicks through the show.
It's like Cubist colorist painting techniques,
coating bodies in street graffiti. *Attitude*
Alvin—break, ballet, dance, history.

**Morning Prayer
(for my father)**

When the flocks vanish,

when the stars dim,

when the mountains scatter,

dawn breaks darkness.

Heaven is cleft.

The voice in my soul

whispers in the clouds.

For the rabbit that screams
on Strivers' Row:
There's a carrot field growing
in your eyes;
Miles blows softly
in your ears,
with a promise.

For the child trapped in the
psych ward:
Doses of drugs and electric shocks
try to break your innocence,
but healing can occur
in a journal entry, a poem,
a simple sentence.

For the lover who swings and salsas
to abusive beats:
Rhythms in an African dance
can rejuvenate your soul,
and you may find
love is your essence.

For the woman who greets death:
Draw life scenes;
your blood is chilled,
but your appetite for living
is stronger than a lions
virgin kill.

As ferocious as a lion

without a catch,

I hunger for milk.

Rain

Drip. Drop.
Showers wet and cold
April tears won't stop
Until they freeze my soul.

It turns my heart to steal
For I am locked in my room
Like a prisoner without a deal
Hoping the sun comes soon.

Flower Girl

Everybody can't
be a begonia, short, low
to the ground, pink, white.

I'm a sunflower,
tall, brown in blossom, steady,
seeds full, edible.

unorthodox man

oooooh brother man,
outrageously beautiful mess,
out beyond melodies,
our bodies mingle
oxygen. Breathe me.
hummmmmm…

Redemption

My earth quakes and shatters.
Life crashes in like a waterfall,
waking every corner of my soul,
but there is no promise
of sunrise.

Do you know joy?
My heart whispers asking me
the same question that it asked
five years ago when I was
clutched in fear with another.

Do you know joy?
the question haunts,
once again, sneaks between
the sheets, seeps in my mind
and alerts my heart:
"Sex is a quick fix."

Do you know joy?
I shut my eyes to avoid
the question, but darkness
forces the answer
to my lips,
"No."

The "no" is louder than
the one that escapes me.

The truth burns and I slip out
of bed into my T-shirt. Crumpled
in a corner, I gasp for breaths.
The penetrating message:
"I don't have joy."

I walk to the mirror,
study my face,
and my Spirit speaks:
"Rest in me;
I will get you there."

I am

awkward when

we hold hands.

My steps are full,

yet somehow simple.

Dare I smile?

Portraits of a Woman Relating

Moon-woman,

a body in motion,

stands still

and slings words

into orbit

like Rumpelstiltskin

spinning gold.

I am here

tasting tender torches

from her tongue.

Feline Friend

My strength is mystical,
like a cat.
I flounder in mid-air,
yet land on my feet.

You are an activity,
in my consciousness
and I'm digging it.
I let go of my soul-fears
masked behind surface beauty,
trade in my logical keys
so that you can see me.

Silly commandments,
like not saying I love you
until I am sure that
you love me too,
do not work--
as we are,
floating in spaces
where I can explore

who I am?

We meet;
life is cold
like chattering teeth
and I am hungry for love.

With no belief,
tangled in poverty,
ill from romantic comedies,
tired as God must have been
on the seventh day,
I really have no idea

how to pray?

In the moments we speak,
spiritual strength multiply by two.
My soul salutes then splits
to become part you.
Just knowing you care
releases answers to billions of
 "God, please send me someone to love"
prayers.

My eighth life ends;
my ninth begins
in a night of ecstasy
and the days we
walk as friends.

Feeling like
lightning on a dark ocean front,
a cold current in calm waters,
a phone ringing in an empty room
shoes walking with no destination.

A silence within made me forget.
Your laughter made me remember.

Katrina Unfinished

The levee is breaking.
Damn!
Weep!

Katrina,
the world watches.
Erupt!

Hundreds turn thousands
displaced,
dysfunctional,
dead.

In two
months
what will
we say...

> *black daughter*
> *took a sip of love's water*
>
> *down in New Orleans,*
> *you know what I mean.*
>
> *you'd be surprised*
> *the color of her eyes.*
>
> *oh yeah,*
> *say it wasn't fair.*

41

Slipped

The landscape has changed.
The oil palm tree is
gone. African greys[3] are mute.

I lost my color strolling
in daylight searching
for the moon.

I slipped, fell in the abyss,
dropped time, whispering
salats[4] for peace.

I quaked, soaking in the Nile,
a lost confused daughter
slipped into the abyss.

---

[3]African grey parrots   [4]Salats: Islamic prayers

Colette

Our birth mother lives, but we are orphans.
The connection is the continent.
We lose our native tongue but do not mourn.
We simply convert the master's dialect.
In Britain, your voice emerges; patios--
your song. In America, Ebonics
will portray my people's vernacular.
Seas have separated us and we feel
no loyalty. It's hard to reunite.
You chopped sugar cane; it's cotton for me.
We might get caught up in a silly fight
about which was more valuable. Uncanny!
Division builds between the two of us.
One category on the census is not enough.

The divide is great between you and me.
I'm Southern fried; you're Curried style, but
we're chicken. And, it's possible, maybe
that we've let our fears dominate what
little space we have to exchange the truth.
I laugh at your inability to match "bright colors!"
And, you see me as so uptight and spooked
about slavery and, "Yankee!" you mutter.
Insults are simple recipes to flame fears. Truce!
Let's be cookbooks with meals like southern fried
jerk chicken, rice and black eyed peas; claim
sisterhood over rum cake and java. It hurts
to always dine alone.

In Jamaica Queens, I meet Colette
from Kingston, Jamaica and we transform beliefs.
Dressed in a black and white polka dot top,
jeans and polka dot socks; desperately matched
to fit in for the first day at school, I flop!
But chatter with Colette on my way home
reveals that she lives close. Eventually,
there are overnight stays. She loves *Buju Banton.*
I worship *Q-tip.* It's reggae Sundays
and rap beats. We're like turntables of fun.
I teach Colette how to electric slide,
She wiggles her waist, I learn how to wind.
When we get angry and our wills collide
 "Respect," she yells! "Chill out," I sigh.
Months later and countless dollar-van rides,
we're still home-girls. Holla!

Confidence

Crumpled on the floor waiting for me,
a dirty ring around her neck, she sleeps.
Then, bleached, pressed, worn with a skirt,
she didn't get the job and is a bit hurt:

my same old buttoned down shirt.

She stands starched at attention,
shouting, "me." Then she enters
Stirring the candidate competition,
in a suit with slacks, the winner:

my same old buttoned down shirt.

She partners with a nerd flicking a pen.
Her tail is tucked neatly into jeans, but
glasses pop out of the pocket seam
where morning coffee stains set in:

my same old buttoned down shirt.

She loves any neck accessories:
Windsor knot or bow tie precision,
colorful beads to break monotony,
pearls of passion perfumed to party:

my same old buttoned down shirt.

With the loosening of the top two
buttons, "pick a boo" bosoms flirt,
silently sealing the deal. In lieu
of dessert, she dazzles as she works:

my same old buttoned down shirt.

Church-hopping

MamMaw baptizes me; the water is cold.
I speak tongues; get the Holy Ghost in the church.

Three boys line up to kiss me at the revival.
My aunt watches from the window in the church.

The story of Adam and Eve is narrated again;
I let go of my sexual hang-ups in the church.

I cry when I hear that, *in the sixties, four girls*
in Sunday School were blown up in the church.

I choreograph *Women of Grace,* working
mothers who dance on Easter in the church.

Proper etiquette stops me cold in *The Cathedral.*
I hate styled hair and fancy clothes in the church.

New Year's Eve sermon spews past midnight;
I am peeved at Pastor Poe in the church.

Broke-up with my man; lost my job that week.
I attend noon prayer daily and sulk in the church.

MamMaw, the evangelist, suffers from dementia.
I cry out to Jesus; rebuke my woes in the church.

Restless

I'm sitting
In my room
In all my silence,
No TV telling,
Computer humming,
Music drumming, or
AC coughing out air.
The noise is in my head,
Loud like
Bombs blowing
Up small towns.

Shhh! Don't Talk About That!

I whisper it 'cause of
my embarrassment and think:
How shameful!

This is some bullshit!

A spoken word teacher,
an educated preacher,
a "you better say what you got to
say and get some attitude"
type of leader
who fights for choices
is stunned voiceless.

Suffocating kisses
ripping my innocence,
turning me into the
rubber-legged dancer.
I can write ten poems on
that and they'd all fall flat
'cause there're really no
words for a punk attack.

I try to handle it like Maya
'cause I've admired her since
I was ten—her mute healing—
but Mississippi God Damn;
I feel more like Nina when

it comes to this injustice.
I disconnect from Christianity;
the spirit-led part of me splits in two
and the vindictive side shouts "Fuck
You!" And I wonder if Jesus, who's still
my best friend, ever just
felt like *Mississippi God Damn,*
'cause my caged bird gets irate, curses, spits,
mutters shit, shit, shit, does her own thing,
loses it completely, almost dies;
but then lets out one huge cackling cry.

I spit up words until I'm heard
And then my birds sing...

black daughter
took a sip of love's water

down in New Orleans,
you know what I mean.

you'd be surprised
the color of her eyes.

oh yeah,
say it wasn't fair.

Wrapped Attention

Mouth dry and slightly open,
in wrapped attention, I listen
to my father:

> *The clouds are gathering*
> *and yes there've been a couple of*
> *raindrops but the storm is*
> *not coming. It's out there*
> *in the distance.*
> *There are things you must do:*
> *take care of yourself,*
> *take your medicine.*
> *If you need help you have*
> *to ask for it 'cause*
> *I'm here for you, baby.*
> *If you ride a horse,*
> *I will trot alongside.*
> *If you fall off,*
> *I'll pick you up,*
> *put you back on.*
> *If the rain comes*
> *I will be your umbrella.*

Beer

Belly up! I ain't no drunk.
I swallow after rush hour.
My week ends.

"Touch down!" they shout.
I swizzle a cold one.
It's a part of the game.

"Alcohooooooolism!"
Charges the accusing finger.
"A cold one," I order.

Moderation's my motto.
His memory is a guilt trip.
I sip one at the party.

So, what's his addiction?
"I wonder 'bout that one,"
Whew! I hail a taxi.

Star Stuck

All's fair in Hollywood.
Lights! Mysterious girl,
we can shape your look.

Blonde bone straight weave,
Camera! Ready! Prostitute
your craft: be bodacious,

and petite, the model type,
right for every scene.
Action! Play the stereotype.

Don't use too much personality.
We need another idol
to encourage insecurities.

Swell the existing societal
eating disorder mess;
boost pharmacy business.

Psychiatrist passing tissues
at the clinic. You got HIV,
neighborhood cracked-out issues?

Great! Reality shows or scary
movies with you playing
the role for you by them.

Flip that script! Show some soul!
Look beyond the powdered nose,
and whitened teeth to

Swahili beauty--intelligent,
sorrowful, angry and jubilant,
unpredictable, unedited, mixed.

In a theater on the screen
I had a dream: portraits of my color,
Hollywood reflected my humanity.

Confused Blue

I pray for instant death,
and just when I get
close to lost breath,
I beg for life, for whatever
is left. Confused blue,
nothing worse than
a confused blue
slanted smile, no real laugh,
damaging depression. Voodoo
vacations to the Caribbean doctor
won't help me be a little less lost,
a little more me. So I remember that
memory is selective, and I chose
to believe that the person I am
is not so different from
the person before the diagnosis.

Healing Time

There was a scar
and I wanted to pick
at it; the temptation
to dig was great.

I remember the knife,
blood-soaked, dripping.
Band-Aids didn't help;
I got a stitch.

Healing was slow.
Most days I resisted
the itch but once
I scratched.

The wound bled
but the pain
was not as intense
as the first cut.

Days passed;
the blemish faded
into the color
of my skin. I win.

Metamorphose

She is a healer.
Friends are accessories
to killing time.

The match does not work.
So she dismisses them
from her light.

She spins a web
around death and begins to
breathe lavishly.

She, who could never smell,
inhales the sweetness of a
honeysuckle.

She, who does not dance,
swirls naked in the sun.
Awake! It is her birth.

Pleasure

Pressing my hips with a kiss,
I whiff your stomach scent.
At night I miss you most. I cope.

Encouraging me, kissing my neck,
Spice in your eyes and I sweat.
At night I miss you most. I wrote.

Sharing a chocolate chip cone,
Tickling-touches and I cuddle close,
At night I miss you most. I bolt.

I'm like a leaf on the lake,
You are water carrying me safe,
At night I miss you most. I float.

Ode to Ice Cream

I
come upon
eternity in flavors:
Chocolate Chip and
Vanilla Bean.
Resting, I enjoy
an addictive peace.
My welts cool.

Release!

I find you in the local bodega
on the corner of 226th Street
passing time, among Italian Ices.
You, worth the weight
and, all the way home I sing:
"Coffee ice cream."

My cure for depression,
my secret nightly obsession.
I'm so committed—
I bake a pie, warm
and pile you on top, high.

The Gifted Quiet

Morning Psalms

(My father, who claims Islam as his religion, calls me every morning and I share a random Psalm from the Bible. He then shows me with words of wisdom how that Psalm applies to his life. After about a year of this routine, I began to use one word from our morning devotion as the springboard to write a poem. The result is this journey through the Psalms. Thank you, Dad.)

Tremble
(Psalms 77:18)

Lightning cracks a red sky.

Thunder shakes. Bodies quake.

Touched by brilliance,

I dance a nameless joy.

Tender
(Psalms 102:4)

In a backward

whimsical wind,

soothing snowflakes

sail gently to

my warm tongue.

Commune
(Psalms 77:6)

When hearts fly

to new moons in June,

periwinkles pray.

Open
(Psalms 34:15)

Morning Glories open

A precious promise,

A wild will,

A dawning desert,

A trouble to heal.

Nation
(Psalms 86:9)

Naked and neutral in humanity,
until a silly side kick
paints a picture of profanity
that locks me in color division.

"Science proved that the first beings
were people of color," she says.
True, but what's the meaning?
Does it keep your humanity in tack?

I need no reminder that I am black.
Every day, the mirror tells me that
I am aching in a nation
with too many color creations.

I'd rather live my life in a rainbow
than in a dedication to the past.
I want to move forward in a flow
where I let go—free to really see.

Color does not indicate destiny.
It has no value to open minds,
imagination and flights of fancy.
That's what God told me.

Inequity
(Psalms 103:3)

The destruction of a people by a monarch:
which was worse—slavery or the holocaust?

"What does she think?" a classmate fumes, calls
to me, the only African American in the room.

I was attempting to avoid the silly dispute about
which genocide was the worst. With a scowl,

I replied, "If I were to add anything to this debate
I'd say, Native Americans roll in a mass grave.

"They're not here to add a comment and
protest the atrocities heaped on their land."

Trust
(Psalms 37:5)

In first days when every impression is about
impressing
and we are saying what we think is right to say,

when our hearts are pulsating in our own truths
and
we have no time to lick other people's wounds,

when speechless in the thickness of someone
claiming
to be witness to words we did not speak, we

finally let go and see the sister we never really got
to know.
We free spirits of trust and come home. Shalom.

Sing
(Psalms 9:2-3)

Sometimes

I can't hear

your chords

but I sing

with love

wrapped around my shoulders.

Marvel
(Psalms 98:1)

I spring

in inexplicable joy

in greenhouse

mother earth

filled with

toxic waste.

Path
(Psalms 16:11)

Fork in a road—
anxious eyes
frame the future,
create conclusions
naked and cold.

Fork in a road—
a heart punches
faded memories
of Grandma Grace,
all money spent,
poor emptied purse.

Fork in a road—
pressure builds;
former friends
move away;
they seek hordes
of happiness
in a world of woes.

Fork in a road—
I hear my God
guide me with
a calm command:
"Let all else go
and take my hand."

Within Me
(Psalms 103:1)

A love I could not imagine,

from a God that I questioned,

has released me from a prison

of shattered innocence and made

it easier to inhale the warmth

of true friendship.

Restore
(Psalms 51:8)

Intoxicated by sunrise, I let

loose with melody in my eyes.

Sad symphony—once my only

song—surges in jubilance to

dissolve my disguises. Eternal

cycle: molding myself in the dark

and restoring insight by light.

Ageless in age, I live to see day.

Salvation
(Psalms 25:5)

Deliverance: rescue, recovery, escape;
Unimaginable mission achieved as you wait.

The God whom you have trusted for truth
Is teaching, leading and preserving you.

Don't fret when passion smashes you into
painful storms of anger and grunts of youth.

Salvation can start with a whisper and awake
with deliverance: rescue, recovery, escape.

Praise
(Psalms 66:8)

Not because I pray five times a day,

nor because I memorize Bible verses, but

it comes unexpectedly while I sing wild like

a child. I lift my voice and lend my ear

to echoes of easy gifts of praise.

A New Song
(Psalms 103:3-4)

My prayer is my praise. My prayer is my praise.
He works it out every day. His skills do amaze.
His truth is in my soul. His virtues I do extol.

I learn divine chords, for He is my reward.
This is the awesome truth: He spared my youth.
Now, I'm in a new phase. I love Him always.

My prayer is my praise. My prayer is my praise
He works it out every day. His skills do amaze.
His truth is in my soul. His virtues I do extol.

The Gifted Quiet

Acknowledgements

I give honor to God for the grace that operates in my life. He blessed me with people who have been sources of astounding support and inspiration. I am especially appreciative of the powerful influences of my mother and my father and of dear family friends: Rosa Parks, Elaine Steele and Toni Parks.

The seeds of *The Gifted Quiet* were planted in my Master's thesis, guided by the creative genius and steady hands of Professors Marilyn Hacker and Pamela Laskin of The City College of New York. The project was watered by memories: some told to me, some my own. It was nurtured by the insightful comments of Jack Estes and the editorial critiques of Bessie W. Blake. Hours of technical support were provided by John Banks and James Carter. My gratitude is immeasurable for the role each of these wonderful and talented individuals played in bringing this volume to publication.

The Gifted Quiet

About the author

RiShana Blake, adjunct professor in the Theater Department at The City College of New York, is Founder and Artistic Director of PureLit Production—a small company that hosts intimate artist showcases and networking events. She has appeared in venues throughout New York City and has sponsored performance workshops and artistic showcases for various youth programs such as Expressions in the Bronx and the VIP program in Queens.

RiShana holds a BA in English from Syracuse University, an MFA in Creative Writing from The City College of New York. She was awarded a scholarship to the Bear River Writers Conference and was chosen as a participant in the Spring 2011 Cave Canem Workshop. Her work has appeared in *Poetry in Performance*, *Promethean*, and *Audience*. She is also a frequent jurist of new artistic expressions.

The Gifted Quiet

CPSIA information can be obtained
at www.ICGtesting.com
Printed in the USA
FSOW01n0627200417
33250FS

9 780983 569978